Ferrets as Pets

A Handy Ferret Owner Guide

Ferrets General Info, Purchasing, Care, Cost, Keeping, Health, Supplies, Food, Housing, Grooming, and More Included!

By: Lolly Brown

Copyrights and Trademarks

All rights reserved. No part of this book may be reproduced or transformed in any form or by any means, graphic, electronic, or mechanical, including photocopying, recording, taping, or by any information storage retrieval system, without the written permission of the author.

This publication is Copyright ©2019 NRB Publishing, an imprint. Nevada. All products, graphics, publications, software and services mentioned and recommended in this publication are protected by trademarks. In such instance, all trademarks & copyright belong to the respective owners. For information consult www.NRBpublishing.com

Disclaimer and Legal Notice

This product is not legal, medical, or accounting advice and should not be interpreted in that manner. You need to do your own due-diligence to determine if the content of this product is right for you. While every attempt has been made to verify the information shared in this publication, neither the author, neither publisher, nor the affiliates assume any responsibility for errors, omissions or contrary interpretation of the subject matter herein. Any perceived slights to any specific person(s) or organization(s) are purely unintentional.

We have no control over the nature, content and availability of the web sites listed in this book. The inclusion of any web site links does not necessarily imply a recommendation or endorse the views expressed within them. We take no responsibility for, and will not be liable for, the websites being temporarily unavailable or being removed from the internet.

The accuracy and completeness of information provided herein and opinions stated herein are not guaranteed or warranted to produce any particular results, and the advice and strategies, contained herein may not be suitable for every individual. Neither the author nor the publisher shall be liable for any loss incurred as a consequence of the use and application, directly or indirectly, of any information presented in this work. This publication is designed to provide information in regard to the subject matter covered.

Neither the author nor the publisher assume any responsibility for any errors or omissions, nor do they represent or warrant that the ideas, information, actions, plans, suggestions contained in this book is in all cases accurate. It is the reader's responsibility to find advice before putting anything written in this book into practice. The information in this book is not intended to serve as legal, medical, or accounting advice.

Foreword

Ferrets belong to the family of skunks, and because they are close relatives, they also have the same musky characteristics! Their musky odor might be one of the reasons why people do not really like ferrets. However, ferrets are known to be one of the greatest pets you can ever own.

They started out to be hunters of rabbits and other rodents in the village. However, due to their great personalities, their functions have greatly changed. Now, the ferret is one of the chosen pets for households. They have a big attitude that would surely tire you out! Due to their personality, they are very easy to train and can learn new commands easily. Who would not want a pet like that?!

Table of Contents

Chapter One: Introduction 9

Chapter Two: History and Basic Characteristics 11

    Where do Ferrets Originated? 13

    Traces of Ferret Domestication 15

        Usage throughout History 16

        Other Important Usage of Ferrets 23

Chapter Three: Turning Ferrets into Pets 29

    Things to Consider When Buying a Ferret 30

    What Age to Get a Ferret? 35

    How Many Ferrets Should I Get? 36

    Jils or Hobs? 37

    Buying a Healthy Ferret 38

    Litter Training 40

    Ferret - Proofing Your Home 41

    Why is a Ferret Right For You? 45

        Temperament 46

        Entertainment 46

    Ease of Care 47

    Are You Ready? 49

Chapter Four: Acquiring a Ferret 55

    A Healthy Ferret 56

A Healthy Ferret Checklist 62

Putting the Facts Together 67

Ready Your Home for the Storm 70

Buying Your Pet Ferret 74

Chapter Five: Housing Requirements for Your Ferret 77

Ferret Proofing 101 78

Ferret - Proofing Your Garden 90

Climbing 101 90

Tips 93

Chapter Six: Food and Nutrition for Your Pet Ferret 99

Ferret Nutrition 101 100

What and When Will My Ferret Eat? 100

What if I Can't Find Ferret Specific Food? 101

Are There Any Food I Can Give My Pet Ferret? 102

Any Foods To Avoid? 102

Varied Health to Have Healthy Body 103

Watch Out For the Hairballs 104

Smart (and Healthy) Treats 105

Chapter Seven: Ferret Grooming 101 107

Brushing Teeth 108

Cleaning Ears 109

Clipping Nails 110

Bathing 111
Photo Credits 113
References 114

Chapter One: Introduction

Ferrets are known to be hunters are first, they would burrow into small spaces and get rabbits to stop infestation in certain farms and barns. They have a nasty habit of even eating their prey. They like to sneak up on rodents and collect them as yummy treats. Because of this trait, they were used by companies to stop rodent infestation in their areas.

Time flew by and their usage changed from a hunter, they became a domesticated pet! Many people do not really believe that a ferret could go well as a household pet.

Chapter One: Introduction

Ferrets have a nasty trait avoided by all - their musky odor that they tend to spread out. But, owners reflected that the odor was only emitted when your pet is scared or if it feels like there is a problem or hazard in the area.

Another great trait of this pet is that it loves to cuddle. It can give you much affection that you would truly crave for! You could spend all day giving and receiving love from this furry creature!

What are you waiting for? This pet ferret is basically for those people who aim for companionship without the big burden of too much training. You just need to set up a great space for it to play in and you are good to go.

Among all things that you need, you should be able to study your pet ferret thoroughly. You should get to know your pet before you decide to buy it. Do intensive research on the pros and cons, as well as the food it needs and how to groom it properly. You should not go into the battle unarmed. Although they are small creatures, your pet ferret surely has a big personality and we hope you can handle it! This book will help you discover the great world of ferrets - enjoy!

Chapter Two: History and Basic Characteristics

Pets, people purchase or adopt them to have companionship in their lives. They might even have pets to have a great addition to their family. Most people prefer having cats or dogs as their household pets as they are very easy to take care of.

However, why not take the risk and discover some new kind of pet? Why not own a then hunter but now a cuddly little creature? Would not you be amazed when this little furry creature would creep up to you and cuddle you

Chapter Two: History and Basic Characteristics

endlessly? And imagine, you could train this kind of pet to do almost any imagine tasks for a pet? If you want to own this pet, go out and get yourself a pet ferret!

Traditionally, your pet ferret is used as a hunter way before. Due to its primitive traits, it would go out and hunt rodents and rabbits. It is smart enough to sneak into small spaces and even tubes and formulate a way to capture the rabbit. Smart, right?

They started out to be best friends of hunters, but now, they are best friends of human beings! Discover the colorful yet history of this one of a kind pet.

People often veer away from this kind of pet; however, we should always keep an open eye to new possibilities of having a ferret as your own household pet. This chapter will help you deal with everything you need about your pet ferret. We hope that you will enjoy this fun - filled journey of owning your very first pet ferret.

The next sections will give you a deep insight on the rich history as well as its basic usage from then and now.

Chapter Two: History and Basic Characteristics

Where do Ferrets Originated?

Our beloved ferret has been a great member of the household of humans for a thousand years now. In today's society, they are considered to be the true companion or humans and they are greatly loved in the entire world.

Mustela putorius furo, or the domestic ferret, is known to be a domesticated Eastern or Western European polecat. The Steppe or Eastern European polecat, also known as Mustela eversmanni, and Mustela putorius putorius, or the Eastern European polecat have great similarities in terms of physical appearance and even its skeletal structure.

This animal can breed and produce offspring with either of the aforementioned species of the polecat. Remember, the domesticated ferret is not the same as the black-footed ferret, also called as the Mustela nigripes, which resides in the western part of the Unites States. The latter kind of ferret was recently reclassified from extinct, but is now being reintroduced again through breeding programs.

Chapter Two: History and Basic Characteristics

Mustela is derived from the Latin word 'mus' which means mouse. Animals belonging in the Mustela genus include mouse catchers and weasels. On the other hand, putorius is derived from the Latin term putor which means stench. The 'stench' this refers to is the odor of the ferret. Lastly, the word 'Furo' comes from the Latin root 'furonem' which means 'thief'. All in all, the ferret can be described as a mouse-catching, smelly, thief animal!

There are still some talks over the specific specie of polecat in which the domesticated ferret actually belongs to. There are several studies performed to fully compare the coat color, behavior, and the skull structure among the three aforementioned species.

Also, there is a little trace of evidence which would tell us when these ferrets were domesticated, as well as how it travelled all the way to Europe. A reason for this little evidence might be due to their tiny bones, rapid decay, or the archaeologist might have treated the remains of these animals as insignificant and did not record any findings from these animals.

Chapter Two: History and Basic Characteristics

Some researchers argue that the ancestors of the modern day ferret actually came from the Northern Africa then were brought to Europe through the Norman and the Roman invasions. Many people also believe that the promulgation of ferrets in Europe was due to the widespread of the rabbits that they have hunted.

Traces of Ferret Domestication

The evident piece of animal domestication is through the remnants of the juvenile characteristics of the species. The characteristics are retained through the selective breeding which makes it more docile and can be easily manipulated by the man.

There are a lot of students done to show the difference in terms of behaviors of the ferrets and wild polecats. These studies are done to show that there is an alteration of the animal's behavior.

Generally, the ferrets are less fearing to the man and show less fear to an unfamiliar environment unlike the polecats. Other than that, ferrets need a lot of time to get used to repetitive noise they have in their surroundings

Chapter Two: History and Basic Characteristics

unlike the wild ferret. This is great evidence that there is a great retention of juvenile responses.

It is very worthwhile to note that if you have separated a wild polecat from its mother before it can open its eyes and then raise by a human, the polecat would be tamed and be imprinted to the human. The polecats would remain tame if there is a continued contact with humankind.

On the other hand, weasels and minks may become tame for short period of time if they are hand reared, but they would then go back to their fearful wild state after its maturity.

The aforementioned behavior, the one being hand-raised, may be the answer on why the ferrets should be domesticated as pets.

Usage throughout History

The ferret was first mentioned by Greek authors, these authors are Aristotle in 350 BC and Aristophanes in 450 BC. However, these references are very unclear because the descriptions matching the animals were missing.

Chapter Two: History and Basic Characteristics

Between the periods of 63 BC and the 24 AD, Strabo has written that there was a plague of rabbits in the islands of Balearic found in the Mediterranean, this plague has caused a famine in the island. Strabo has described this animal as of Libyan in origin. Its main purpose was to hunt and they were muzzled then put into the rabbit holes. This ferret-like animal would then cause the rabbits inside to bolt from the hole, outside of which the dogs and men were ready to capture it.

The aforementioned practice has a great resemblance to the ferret practice that was taking place in Europe for a couple of centuries now. Authors Isidore of Seville in 600 AD and Pliny in 23-79 AD has mentioned that ferrets were used to hunt rabbits.

Ferrets were also believed to be used in household to control rodents, but almost all the references could easily relate to rabbits and ferrets.

The mongoose, the ferret's close cousin, was primarily used to control snake and rodent. This practice is continued to this day, especially those in indigenous areas.

Chapter Two: History and Basic Characteristics

These references to ferret-like creatures has paved the way for hypothesis that this specie has originated in the Mediterranean area, however, there are insufficient evidences to fully support this claim.

In the 1200, the ferret has spread in Germany. There are some tales that stated that Genghis Khan may have utilized these ferrets in 1221 in Afghanistan. In England, the first reference for the ferret was in 1223, and it was again referenced in 1281. There was a ferreter in the Royal Court in the latter year.

In the late 1200s up to the late 1300s, there is other information that came from England. In a story, you need around forty shillings to own a ferret. Another story states that ferrets were only owned by high-ranking church officials. In 1384, King Richard II has issued a decree to allow his clerk to use ferrets to hunt down rabbits. In 1390, King Richard has issued a decree to stop using the ferrets on Sundays.

Gerner from Zurich has given the description of the first albino ferret. In 1551, he said that the ferret is "the color of wool stained with urine." From this point forward, there

Chapter Two: History and Basic Characteristics

are a lot of evidences pointing out to using ferrets to hunt rabbits.

Until the 20th century, the fur production from ferrets was very less popular. During the 18th century, ferrets were used in ships to control the rodent breakout. We can also deduce that humans enjoyed the ferret's personality and kept these little creatures as lifetime companions. We can conclude that ferrets were primarily used to hunt rabbits. They were used to control pests as well as sports.

There are some evidences that ferrets were used to hunt rabbits by the Roman soldiers. There are some speculations that it was due to the expansion of the Roman Empire that there is a great spread of Ferrets in the Northern European continent. While some people believe that ferrets have spread due to the Norman invasions.

One thing is clear, where there are rabbits, there are also ferrets. The European rabbit, the founding fathers of the common household rabbits, were originally from the Iberian Peninsula in Spain. These animals had been captively raised for around 2000 years. In Northern Europe, rabbits were introduced alongside the ferrets.

Chapter Two: History and Basic Characteristics

New Zealand colonizers imported rabbits as game animals in the 1860s. Around the 1870s, rabbits were ruining the landscape in New Zealand because there were no predators that could stop and control these creatures.

Around 1879, five ferrets were introduced in New Zealand to control the population of the rabbits. After this scene, the government has released thousands of ferrets around 1882 to 1886. Weasels and stoats are also released in New Zealand. These animals are close family members of the ferret. Due to this incident, Ferrets developed many colonies in New Zealand. However, this act did not eradicate the rabbits, but it contributed to the decline of native birds. The ferrets happily coped in the wild because the climate in the country is very ideal. Other than that, ferrets really had no predators other than man.

There are many flightless birds in New Zealand and because there were many predators, such as the ferrets, the birds are at a great risk of dying. However, ferrets are not the biggest factor for the loss of the birds in the country, but, the presence of these animals greatly impacted the birds. Today, there are around one million ferrets in New Zealand.

Chapter Two: History and Basic Characteristics

In Australia, the rabbits were primarily introduced by the British settlers. The reason for the introduction was just like in New Zealand; however, the consequences in New Zealand and Australia are the same. As a solution, they welcomed ferrets to control the problem. Unfortunately, ferret can't really build good colonies due to difference in climates and other existing predators such as feral cats, fox, hawks, and dingoes.

Recently, there is a decrease in the usage of ferrets to hunt rabbits, controlling rodents, or even in fur production. They are now commonly known to be household pets. These animals are even kept as pets in Japan and South Africa, as well as almost all parts of Europe.

United States of Ferrets!

In the 18th century, the ferrets were introduced to the US through ships that carried them. Other than that, ferrets were introduced as hunting companions.

In the 1900s, ferrets were welcomed to the country in high quantity to use as 'vermin' exterminators. Ferrets were used to destroy racoons, rabbits, rats, gophers, and mice.

Chapter Two: History and Basic Characteristics

Prey usually hides when they smell the 'scent' of the ferret. This has caused the ferrets to protect warehouses, granaries, and barns. Ferrets were also used to control rodents, as promoted by the USDA.

You can call the ferretmeiste to release ferrets in your farm, if you think your property is infested. These ferrets would search and destroy the vermin especially when they try to escape. Big companies even keep a number of ferrets to prevent infestation of pests. However, when there is a boom in rodenticides, ferrets were not really needed and this task died down eventually.

Unlike in other counties, United States did not really like the idea of fur farming. In most states, hunting with ferrets was made illegal in the 20th century.

By the mid-20th century, Americans have now embraced the idea of having ferret as companion. This is the primary role of the ferrets in the United States. Currently, there is no count for the feral ferret population. The only kind of ferret introduced in the country was the domesticated kind and not the wild polecat.

Chapter Two: History and Basic Characteristics

Other Important Usage of Ferrets

There are usages of ferrets in different parts of the world. These are:

Rabbit Hunters

- ✓ One of the first historical use of domesticated ferret
- ✓ This may be the main reason for the domestication of the ferrets.
- ✓ The act of using the ferret is called ferreting.
- ✓ The main usage of ferrets before was obtaining meals for humans and even population control of the rabits.
- ✓ In hunting rabbits, there is actually little to no training for ferrets, because they like running around the burrows to seek out their prey.
- ✓ During the ancient times, people put muzzles of the ferret to prevent killing and eating of the rabbit while underground.
- ✓ There is some evidence that shows that owners put holes in the lower and upper lips of the animal to tie the lips together, or even place a metal ring so the lips would be shut together during the hunt.

Chapter Two: History and Basic Characteristics

- ✓ Do not be afraid, these muzzles are not used today. In lieu of this apparatus, a harness with a long line is usually used.
- ✓ The shutting of the mouth would prevent rabbit from bolting out the hole before it ever gets caught.
- ✓ Before the ferrets are released in the rabbit holes, the holes are covered with nets that are placed with stakes. These nets would close when the rabbit would escape.

Rodent Control

- ✓ Ferrets were used as pest control as soon as they became domesticated.
- ✓ Ferrets would hunt birds and even small mammals as part of their diet, especially if they are allowed to hunt within the household.
- ✓ As we have said before, these ferrets were introduced to control rodents around the granaries and barns, especially on the American and European ships.
- ✓ The ferret was the official mascot of the Massachusetts Colonial Navy, organized in December 29, 1775. It was later on reactivated in 1986 and 1967.

Chapter Two: History and Basic Characteristics

Fur Production

✓ Europe had used and raised ferrets for fur production for many centuries.

✓ United States had established the ferret fur production in the early 1900s.

✓ The wild European polecat was bred mainly to maintain the quality and the uniformity of the color of the fur since the people preferred the wild coloring of the ferret.

✓ A fitch coat is what we call a coat made out of ferret fur. Now, there is a cease of practice in making fur using ferrets, eventually, people hope that this practice will soon die down.

Transporters

✓ Due to the willingness and the anatomy of the ferret to run through the dark and long tunnels, the ferrets were a great choice for transporting cable wire through long pipes.

✓ Camera crews, people working in airline jets, oilmen in the North Sea, and the telephone companies have used ferrets for putting up cables in long pipes.

Chapter Two: History and Basic Characteristics

- ✓ The put harness on the ferret, where the thin long nylon line is attached. This line will be connected to a cable that needs to be pulled through the conduit.
- ✓ However, since the development of mechanical device, ferret became obsolete in the task of being a transporter.

Ferret Legging

- ✓ Ferret legging was a popular English pub sport. This sport has been around for a long time, but it is not common anymore.
- ✓ In this sport, the contestant tied his trouser legs around the ankles, then two ferrets would be placed down his pants, then the waist of his trousers will be secured. If the ferret will bite you, this is the only time it can be removed from the pants.
- ✓ The goal of this game is to keep the ferrets inside the pants the longest.
- ✓ A 72-year old man from Yorkshire withstood the angry bites of the ferrets for five hours and 26 minutes in 1983.

Chapter Two: History and Basic Characteristics

Biomedical Research

- In the 20th century, ferrets became good models for biomedical research.
- The first usage of the ferret was to study the human influenza virus, in which these animals are susceptible.
- Right now, ferrets are used in the areas of toxicology, virology, reproductive physiology, pharmacology, physiology, endocrinology, anatomy, and teratology.
- Due to human research, the by - product of these things has helped greatly in understand the ferret physiology, anatomy, and diseases.
- There are a large number of healthy ferrets in different breeding facilities in the United States; because of this, there is a wide use of ferrets in biomedical usage.
- Some countries do not have enough facilities so the ferrets can't be used readily.
- The breeding facility in the United States also yields the biggest ferret percentage to be used as pets.

Companion Animals

- Companionship is the most common use of ferrets today.

Chapter Two: History and Basic Characteristics

- ✓ These animals are easy to care for, entertaining, small, and with great responsive personalities.
- ✓ Ferret are interbred to have a great variety of color, now, there is even a long haired ferret variation.
- ✓ There were several organizations set-up to devote time and resources in nurturing ferrets as pets; this also caused the ferrets to spring all over the world.
- ✓ There are also classes and shows devoted for ferrets. These ferrets compete in being best-dressed, being best in color, racing that involves long tubes and bags, and even a yawing contest.
- ✓ It is truly great that once a working animal, we can surely enjoy ferrets as pet.

These are just some of the basic information about the beloved pet, the ferret. This information will greatly help you in raising, breeding, and taking care of your chosen pet. However, there are still a lot of things that you need to know to fully understand the mechanics of your pet. Read on to know more about this amazing, little creature.

Chapter Three: Turning Ferrets into Pets

We have already covered the background as well as the history of the ferrets. However, this knowledge is not enough to fully understand how these creatures work. Ferrets are great house companions that would surely lighten up any household. There are a lot of things that you need to know about this wonderful creature.

This chapter will cover the reasons why you should own a ferret today. Aside from that, we will deal with all the

Chapter Three: Turning Ferrets Into Pets

things that make up ferrets as pets. Make sure that you go breeze through this chapter to make up your mind whether you want to keep ferrets as pets.

Things to Consider When Buying a Ferret

There are a lot of things that you need to consider before you buy your ferret. These animals are active, playful, loving, and curious creatures. These animals make wonderful pets; however, before you go off and buy this pet, there are things that you need to take note of.

Time

You should only choose a ferret as your pet if you have time with them, especially those who can bond well with these animals. These animals are friendly, quiet, intelligent, inquisitive, and companionable.

At some moments of the day, ferrets are so active and very capable of being in trouble unless they are carefully supervised. It is also noted that ferrets are intelligent, this makes them great companions and they can easily amuse

Chapter Three: Turning Ferrets Into Pets

themselves when the owner is not around. The physical and mental health of the ferrets greatly needs the interaction and attention of their handlers.

Legalities

There are certain legalities in how you own, breed, and even sell a ferret, especially where you live. There are certain regulations which ferrets are heavily involved.

Only neutered males are allowed to be kept as pets in California. In Carson City, Nevada, you are not allowed to own a ferret if you have a small child in your house.

To know the specific regulation in your area, you need to check with the local Fish and Game or Wildlife department, your local vet, or even the humane society. The three aforementioned organizations will also advise you to permit and license your pet properly. In order states, you may need to pay a certain amount to permit or license your pet. The fee for this would reach $15 or even more.

Costs

Chapter Three: Turning Ferrets Into Pets

The typical price of a ferret would vary widely; it could range from $65 up to $250. The purchase of this animal is only the initial cost. Aside from buying these animals, you need to pay another $150 to $350 for vaccinations (such as rabies), basic supplies, and vet examinations.

You also need to set aside a budget for neutering or spaying your pet, you can ask your vet for the price you need to pay before you purchase your pet. You may also want to buy an older, altered animal rather than buying a young animal.

Aside from that, you will also need money for vet care, updating of vaccines, and renewal of licenses. Other than that, you need to give food, as well as litters, deodorizing cleaners, medicines such as hairball remedies, collars, shampoos, leads, and vitamin supplements.

Compatibility

People are naturally concerned on how a ferret would get along and treat other pets and children.

A ferret might be demanding for your child, it needs

Chapter Three: Turning Ferrets Into Pets

careful adult supervision and the maturity of a child. Your child needs to know that the ferret acts different from a cat, dog, and any other pet. Aside from that, your child needs be responsible enough to take care and handle your ferrets. This kind of pet is not recommended in a household with children younger than seven years old, especially those houses with babies or infants.

Ferrets are natural hunters, which mean they can't get along with fish, birds, rodents, rabbits, or even lizards. If you have these pets at home, you need to carefully supervise them at all times. But, your pet could go along well with cats and dogs. However, there are dog and other terriers who are natural hunters, which mean they might be in conflict with your ferret.

If you have a cat or a dog, you need to slowly introduce them to your pet ferret, and vice - verse. You also need to have another person who will hold the dog or the cat and the one to hold the ferret; this act would allow the pets to smell and get to know each other that provides them reassurance and encouragement, your dog or cat might be anxious or bewildered at first, so you need to give them extra attention.

Learn the animals' behavior and see if they are okay. If you believe that the animals respect and accept each other, you can slowly let them interact freely under close supervision. Just make an available escape route for your ferret, just in case. No matter how your pets go well together, you still need to supervise them wherever and whatever they are doing. Have separate feeding are and bowls and do not let your ferret play with the other toys of your other pets.

Aggressiveness

You need to teach your ferret not to bite and nip, just like how you need to teach your puppies and kitties that biting is inappropriate.

If you have a domesticated ferret, it will not be really aggressive or vicious, but naturally, your ferret likes games such as tug-of-war, hunting, mock combat or even chasing.

Your baby ferret do not really know what hurts and what does not hurt, unless you tell it what is and what is not.

Chapter Three: Turning Ferrets Into Pets

You need to be the one to set up the boundaries and rules to your pet, it will be up to you to establish those boundaries, without hurting your pet or mistrust, or even teaching it through fear.

In some cases, your pet might even respond to certain noises, fear, pain, or actions just like biting. You need to alter this behavior through eliminating the noise source. If the noise source is on your need, you need to see the light from the perspective of your ferret. Remember, this behavior is not done by your pet intentionally, or even trying to do it because it is mean.

What Age to Get a Ferret?

Your ferret would retain a lot of its wilderness traits because of this they need care, affection, and understanding. If you can't give enough patience, time, or knowledge of the needs of your pets, you might have a difficult time disciplining your pet. In this scenario, your pet might feel abused or even neglected, you might have to resold or give away your pet. If you want to have older ferrets, you might

Chapter Three: Turning Ferrets Into Pets

encounter these kinds of ferrets in the pound.

If you can't give time and energy to raise a baby ferret, you might want to rescue or adopt an older animal. You just need to know why the pet is abandoned or being given away, and be sure that you can give a good environment for your pet.

If you believe that you can take care of a young ferret, the best age of the pet would be around 8 to 16 weeks; however, some ferrets could be sold as young as six weeks old.

If your ferret is less than eight weeks old, it is not really ready to leave its siblings and mother, so it is best to wait until they reach the twelve weeks old. A young ferret needs more training, time, and patience than a mature ferret, however, it will give you adaptability and playfully, plus it could give you the joy of watching it grow up.

How Many Ferrets Should I Get?

Your ferret might be better living off as a sole companion to you, rather than having playmates. However,

Chapter Three: Turning Ferrets Into Pets

this depends well on the time, companionship, and home environment that you can give. On the other hand, you can also have other ferrets with your pet to provide companionship when you can't give it. Your ferret is very playful, so it needs to have a lot of companionship and interaction. Some people point out that the wild relative of the ferret are solitary animals. While some people say that ferrets love to play one another.

The number of ferrets you want to own is totally up to you, but, if you want to have more than one ferret, make sure that you obtain them at a young age, probably at the same time, and slowly introduce them to one another just like you are introducing a cat or a dog.

Jils or Hobs?

Female ferrets, also called as Jils, and male ferrets, also known as Hobs, have their unique advantages, mainly concerning their reproductive abilities.

If you decide you want to breed your ferret, you need to do a thorough research. On the other hand, if you do not want to breed ferrets, you should spay or neuter your pet.

An unmated, unaltered Jil will be in heat for six month every year; the ferret will have a change in behavior as well as the physical characteristics. The hormones involved in heat greatly increase the risk of stress-related illnesses as well as leukemia. On the other hand, an unaltered male would become too aggressive to other male ferrets during breeding season. You should know this trait if you want to keep more than one ferret inside your house. Neutering could also decrease the smell of the pet.

Buying a Healthy Ferret

The gender, color, and gender of the ferret is not really a big issue when buying a pet ferret, however you should always remember to pick out the healthiest pet from the bunch.

When you pick out your first pet, make sure you choose the one who is in best health. The best way to know the best ferret in the litter aside from judging their appearance and 'cuteness overload factor' is the general behavior of the ferret.

The pet of your choosing should be alert, curious, and playful. The ears should be erect, the eyes must be bright, and the ferret's movement should be supple and smooth. Aside from that, there should be no discharge from the nose, eyes, ears, anus, or any sexual opening. Aside from that, the mouth, ears, and pads should be clean and pink.

Scented or Not?

Healthy ferrets should only have a slight musky odor that comes from a gland found under their skin. They also have a scent sac by their anus, and some of these scents are passed on to their feces to show the other animals the territory of the ferrets.

Hobs have stronger scents in their urine. If you plan to descent your ferret through removing the scent sac will not help to ward of the musky healthy odor but it would lead to a lot of medical problems. However, if you plan to neuter or spay your pet, it would rarely release their scent, unless they are extremely frightened or even agitated. If they ever release the scents, it would dissipate quickly and easily be treated with special solvents or could even evaporate on its own. Aside from that, you should keep the litter box clean to control the odor of the ferret.

Litter Training

Unlike other household animals, ferrets do not really know how to use the litter box. However, you could still train them to use it.

Start the litter training using a corner box near its cage or by a small area. Slowly, allow them more freedom when they continue to use the box. You need to have a small amount of the dirty litter left in the pan to help your pet understand why the litter box is there. You can also discourage your ferret from using other places in the room by covering it with bedding or even food bowls. Make sure you use positive reinforcement words and pet your ferrets and give them treats. Make sure to remove the odor with a bacterial - based odor remover or using some enzymes to remove the mistakes. And you must keep a close eye to your pet until they get a hang of it.

Ferret - Proofing Your Home

Aside from litter training your ferret, you also need to take additional precautions to protect your ferret's safety, as well as the safety of your possession and your home. Your ferret is naturally curious as well as energized, and because of their physiology, your ferret could very much squeeze into small spaces.

Hobs are twice as big as jils, you need to block any holes over the size of 1/2" x 1". Also take good care around cabinets, kitchen appliances, as well as ventilation and heating ducts. Protect and put safety covers over all outlets and electrical cords. Put safe gates on your doorways, you can also use plexiglas or wood to slot the door frames. Make sure to also watch your feet, or your guests' feet wherever you go. Ferret, most of the time, get underfoot unintentionally.

Furniture is another concern of Ferret owners. Ferrets

like to snuggle on nests, so it is best not to allow them on sofas, couches, beds, and even sofa beds. Make sure to fasten thin plywood as well as heavy fabric across the bottoms of sofas, couches, and etc. Do not use futons, because these things are very difficult to safeguard. Also be aware of levers and springs inside the reclining chairs and sofabeds. There may be a need to use a plastic carpet protector over anything that your pet might find very enticing to eat, especially because your pets love to nibble on floor fabrics.

Also note the contents of your cabinets and drawers prevent your pet from ever opening them. Also keep the soaps, cleaners, medicines or other hazardous materials out of your pet's reach. Put down the toilet lid to avoid accidents for your pet. Aside from that, make sure to note the bath tubs, sinks, buckets, and other deep places that you can put water. Aquariums should also have covers to prevent accidental swimming and drowning of your pet.

Also note the interaction of your pet and your ferret. Many house plants are very toxic, dangerous, or even deadly for your pet. You should check your plant at home before you allow your ferret to run free in your house.

Chapter Three: Turning Ferrets Into Pets

To avoid accidental chewing of the plants, you may try coating the leaves with bitter apple or even a similar solution.

Just like any child, cat, or dog, you also need to protect your pet from hazardous materials that could suffocate it, such as drapery cords and plastic bags. Due to the small size of your ferret, you need to consider items in your house such as cardboard tubes that holds the toilet paper, gift wrap, or even paper towel. These may be insignificant toys but they could pose a great danger for your pet.

Toys

Be sure to provide a lot of varied toys for your pet because your pet ferret would surely love to play. The more toys they have, the less mischief they can commit. If they can't find a toy inside their area, they might be tempted to make or even find one! And, it is surely a delight to watch your ferret play.

Most owners prefer giving cat toys for your ferret, but, ferrets are hard players than the regular cats. They would chew more vigorously and the rubber or foam or any other small parts could be lodged inside their windpipes or it might even cause intestinal blockage.

Make sure you buy durable toys, just like ferret tunnels, swings, and hammocks. These things would provide countless hours of excitement for your pet.

Food

Your pet ferret's diet mainly consists of protein and fat, it also needs a lot of fresh water. Some pet owners prefer feeding them kitten or cat food because there are only a number of ferret foods available in the market.

In whatever food you might want to choose, make sure to avoid fish - flavored cat food or fish in general. If you ever feed your ferret fish, it would create foul scent in the litter box. Dog food, on the other hand, would only fill up your ferret but not provide your pet with essential nutrients.

Do not even think of feeding your ferret human snacks, because many of these things are indigestible or even toxic. Do not give caffeine, chocolate, colas, tobacco products, coffee, ice cream, tea, onions, and milk.

Chapter Three: Turning Ferrets Into Pets

Ferrets need variety of food and they will do anything to eat a yummy treat. It could learn a lot of tricks such as walking to heel, sitting up, rolling over, or even begging.

You can also reward your ferret for desirable behavior, or you can introduce fruits, vegetables, and treats to your ferret's diet as a variety. There are also especially formulated ferret treats in great flavors such as peanut butter up to carob raisin.

Why is a Ferret Right For You?

This part will give you an insight of the pros and cons about ferrets. This will help you decide on why you should or you should not buy your Ferret today.

Ferrets can be a wonderful pet that would provide you with endless entertainment due to its intelligence. However, you should not get one instantly. Just like any pet, there are a lot of pros and cons when owning a ferret. There are a lot of ferrets that live in rescue shelter, so if you decide to take home a pet, it is better if you rescue rather than shop.

Chapter Three: Turning Ferrets Into Pets

These are some reasons why ferrets make amazing pets:

Temperament

When you understand how ferrets work, you would instantly fall in love with it. They have great personalities, and owning ferrets would add great joy to your life. If you have socialized as well as handle your ferret well, it will turn into the playful, loving, and inquisitive pet that you would love to have.

Ferrets are also great with children, as long as your child knows not to overexcite or startle your pet, so they should always be supervised when they are playing with each other. Ferrets also easily bond with their owners, so you need to prepare for some snuggles.

Entertainment

Because they are very smart, your ferret could provide you tons of hours of entertainment. You should mingle with your pet for at least two hours every day.

Chapter Three: Turning Ferrets Into Pets

They love to play around; a plus factor is that your pet thinks of you as a toy too. They are highly intelligent and could easily pick up new behaviors - so you can teach and train them to do tricks! If you have more than one ferret, you would also have lots of fun watching two or more ferrets play.

Ease of Care

Ferrets require a great amount every day to take care of; however, they are fairly easy to take care. There are specialized ferret food found on the market, you just need to be in the lookout for these things.

It is also such a breeze to train your ferret to use the litter box; it would make cleaning the cages very easy. They are not really bugged with human interaction within the day and they can go on the day without their humans, so these pets are for the people who are very busy.

Smell

Some people do not really like ferrets because of their

smell, while some people do not really mind the smell. It is not really unpleasant, but they have a musky and strong odor. This smell could be contained in a minimum by cleaning out the cage around 3 or more times a week, or you can do it biweekly or even monthly. However, you should not dry out your ferret's coat by over - bathing.

Destructiveness

Your ferret is naturally curious, it would like to get into anything and they are really afraid to make a mess inside your house. So if you plan to welcome a ferret into any room, you need to have these rooms ferret-proofed.

These ferrets like to scrabble and scratch at the door and they really like to burrow their heads in the sofa. They also like to chew any electrical cables they can get their teeth into, and would likely to squeeze into any small space they can find. You need to constantly guide them inside your house wherever they go to avoid any accidents.

Time

Ferrets will eat up time more than you imagine. It is

best to keep them inside the cages while you are outside or at work, but they need around four hours a day outside of their cage. Another two hours playing with toys or even interacting with them. These pets also need regular grooming such as ear cleaning, nail clipping, and tooth brushing.

Are You Ready?

Ferrets are big responsibility. They have different sets of needs and wants from the common household pets, but that does not mean that you will give other kind of love and treatment to these furry little creatures.

Here are some other things that you need aside from buying the pet ferret. Take these things into consideration, because these things will make your pets happy.

The cage

- You still need a cage for temporary use and training, even if you plan to have your ferret inside of the room.

Chapter Three: Turning Ferrets Into Pets

- You can use multi-level large cages with ramps as the house of these pet ferrets.
- 24 x 24 x 18 in or 60 x 60 x 45 in is the ideal size for one or two ferrets.
- Aquariums are not really great for your pet ferret because of poor air circulation and even inadequate space.
- The cage should be very easy to clean and sturdy enough to withstand the digging that your pet might do.
- You can use a wire or solid mesh with squares as the cage floor to prevent food injuries for your pet.
- The doors should be securely latched with bar spacing to provide great security for your pet.
- Make sure to put the cage away from drafts, sunlight, or even cold damp areas.
- Your ferrets like to hide and burrow, so you need to have a bedding, such as shirts or towels in which your ferret could sleep or curl up to.
- There are also a lot of sleeping materials easily available in the market, such as tents, cloth tubes, and hammocks.

- Make sure that the burrowing material is free from any holes, loops, or any loose strings to prevent the nails from ever getting caught.
- If your ferret has decided to chew on the cloth, remove these items immediately and replace it with a wooden box or a cardboard with clean straw or hay as the sleeping area.

Litter Pans

- You need to litter train your pet once you have get them, especially at a young age.
- Place a small pan on the place where your pet has already selected, this will be called as a 'latrine'
- The second pan should be in the corner in which your pet could exercise.
- In the litter pan, put a thin layer of litter.
- Young ferrets would play around and burrow in clay or clumping litter.
- Recycled newspaper or fiber re great litters because that are more absorbent, cleaner, non - toxic, and compost friendly.

Chapter Three: Turning Ferrets Into Pets

- Ferrets do not know how to cover up their ways, so you need to spot clean the litters daily and change the litter several times a week to eliminate odor.
- If you want your ferret to exercise more often, place the litter box on several parts of the house.

Toys

- Be careful in selecting toys for your ferrets, even though they really like to play.
- Do not give any pet product made out of foam or latex rubber because these things are easily ingested.
- Have tunnel-type toys such as dryer hoses, cardboard mailing tubes, PVC pipes, and paper bags to mimic normal activity such as burrowing.
- You can also give cloth toys but only do this if your pet does not chew on the fabric.
- Remove any eyes and buttons from the cloth toys before you give them to your pet.

Chapter Three: Turning Ferrets Into Pets

- Pick out the toys made out of indestructible materials such as hard plastic, but choose toys that are large enough not to be ingested, such as ping pong balls.

These are some things that you need to have before you even buy your pet. We have also covered the things that you need to consider before you even buy the ferret in the first place.

Chapter Three: Turning Ferrets Into Pets

Chapter Four: Acquiring a Ferret

This chapter will deal with buying your first ferret as a pet. We will help you look for the healthiest ferret from the bunch. Aside from that, we will help you in a step-by-step process into adopting or the purchase of your pet.

Purchasing your first pet is a big step. You need to take time to get to know your pet as well as really get to know why you need a pet inside your house. You should not just want a ferret because it is a good house decoration, you must want a pet to have a lifelong companion that would surely cheer you up in your everyday life.

Chapter Four: Acquiring a Ferret

A Healthy Ferret

People believe that ferrets are mischievous creatures. However, this trait makes them truly exciting to watch. As a fur parent, a way to welcome this healthy pet in your life understands how to keep it healthy and happy throughout its life.

You need to have annual check-ups with vets but you should also know the signs of a healthy ferret. This will ensure you that your pet will have a long, happy, and healthy life.

Eyes

- Looks can somehow be deceiving, this holds true for the eyes of your ferret.
- Physically, they have bright, big eyes, but the ferret eyes are very poor and they tend to have problems with their eyesight.
- We do not have the same color scheme as our beloved pet, and they might have a hard time seeing in bright light.

- Because they have poor eyesight, your ferrets have other heightened senses.
- Hearing, touch, and smell are very acute for ferrets, with this, it is very difficult to note which ferret is sighted or blind.
- Even though the eyes have low functionality, a small scratch or laceration in your pet's eyes is always considered to be an emergency.

Ears

- Your pet ferret has excellent hearing.
- You need to regularly clean the ferret's ears to maintain great hearing ability. Your ferret tends to develop wax in the ear.
- You may need to contact your vet if there is a waxy, dark build up that reappears after you have cleaned your ferret's ears.

Chapter Four: Acquiring a Ferret

Nose

- Your pet ferrets generally follow their noses to decide.
- They use the sense of smell to explore the world around them.
- They are very curious and they try to sniff everything that they come contact into.
- To spot a healthy ferret, your pet must have a moist nose, free from any discharge and scales.
- A simple runny nose could be a serious symptom of a condition that should be checked by the vet immediately.
- Your pet's nose can become dry after some burrowing; however, it should not be a cause of emergency on your part.

Mouth

- Just like a hockey player, your pet may sometime chip or break their teeth.
- You should immediately consult your vet if you see a broken or chipped tooth.

Chapter Four: Acquiring a Ferret

- Do not fret, tooth loss for baby ferrets is fairly common.
- Adult ferrets typically have 40 teeth. They use this to chow down food. When they get older, some of their teeth may turn yellow.
- If there is a tartar build up or even a foul odor coming out of your ferret's teeth, consult the vet immediately for the needed cleaning to have the correct oral health.

Body

- Your pet is very flexible, they turn and twist freely, sometimes, and people think that they do not have any bones.
- Flexibility is one of the innate talents that your pet has. It is noted that your pet could turn its head for 180 degrees, which is very uncommon and unusual for vertebrates.
- This flexibility helps the ferret to crawl through tight spaces; they can fit into almost anything! They can

- even go through a space as small as the size of their heads.
- An adult ferret would weight around three to five pounds. Hobs are heavier than jils, but both have an average length of 14 inches.
- Make sure to regularly check your ferret's body for any bumps, lumps, and anything else that looks different from the ordinary.

Fur

- The hairs are thick just as the ferret's body is thick.
- A healthy ferret will have a glossy and soft texture of coat from head to tail.
- Every ferret is unique; they have different markings or hair color. This makes them endlessly admirable.
- Some pet markings include face masks.
- These animals shed their coats twice a year, so the coat colors change slight with the change the season, so do not be alarmed if there is a change in color.

Chapter Four: Acquiring a Ferret

- You need to weekly brush the coat using a soft brush to keep your pet's coat and skin healthy.
- Note that your pet's fur should be free from any bald spots and soft in texture.

Skin

- Your ferret does not have sweat glands.
- This trait would make your pet easily overheat in temperatures over 85, so you need to avoid places with warmer climates.
- Even though they do not have sweat glands, ferrets have scent glands in which their odors are emitted to.
- You should monthly bathe your pet with a ferret shampoo; this would keep the odor under control.
- Change the bedding and remove the feces daily to control the odor.
- Your pet might also experience itchy, scaly skin, so if you see this condition, immediately consult your vet.
- Regularly check your pet for injuries, fleas, and any other signs of trouble in their skin.

Chapter Four: Acquiring a Ferret

Anus

- Skunks and ferrets are relatives, and it just so happens they share one unwanted characteristic—an anal scent gland. Ferrets only release their scent when scared; however, most ferrets meant to be pets have already been de-scented.

A Healthy Ferret Checklist

The next part of this section will summarize what we have just discussed in the previous pages. This page will be a simple cheat sheet on how to find the best and healthiest ferret in the area:

✓ Eyes:
- Big
- Clear
- Bright
- even in size
- Free of discharge.

Chapter Four: Acquiring a Ferret

- Ears:
    - Should be pink
    - clear of dirt or debris

- Nose
    - Smooth
    - Moist
    - free of scales

- Whiskers
    - Soft
    - Long
    - Full

- Fur:
    - clean, shiny
    - completely covering the body,
    - free of fleas
    - Free of bald spots
    - Free from sores.

Chapter Four: Acquiring a Ferret

- ✓ Skin
  - Smooth
  - not scaly
  - free of lumps
  - no bumps
  - no sores.

- ✓ Body
  - firm
  - The muscle is evenly distributed
  - muscular
  - Athletic

- ✓ Genitals/anus:
  - clean
  - healthy looking
  - not protruding or prolapse
  - with no signs of discharge or feces

Chapter Four: Acquiring a Ferret

- ✓ Feces
  - tubular in shape
  - smooth
  - firm in consistency
  - tan to brown in color
  - Runny and/or discolored feces is a sign of indigestion or serious illnesses

- ✓ Behavior
  - alert
  - curious
  - Playful
  - gentle
  - with a good attitude
  - Young ferrets like to teeth, just like puppies
  - A healthy ferret will appear happy and have a confident attitude.
  - They tend to sleep around 18 to 20 hours a day.

Chapter Four: Acquiring a Ferret

When you get to know your ferret and through observation his daily behavior, you will be able to know when something is wrong about your pet. If you detect the problem early on, your ferret could receive immediate treatment and care that would ensure that your pet would be healthy and happy for many years to come.

When having pets, maybe ferrets are not the first wild animal that crosses your mind. It is really less popular than birds, dogs, cats, and even mice, but ferret owners would brag about their animal's inquisitive and social nature. They would also boast about their ease of upkeep and cleanliness. If you are certain you want to be part of the ferret-owning world, make sure that you do a thorough research first. Find out in this section if both you and your house are ready for owning the ferret.

Chapter Four: Acquiring a Ferret

Putting the Facts Together

Make sure that you have done a research on all the state regulations and the legal requirements when owning a pet ferret.

In some areas, owning ferrets as a choice for pet is quite illegal. Some states in Unites States allow ferrets as pets, but some states, such as in Hawaii and California, are not open to the idea at first.

In Rhode Island, you need to secure a permit first if you want to own a ferret. Make sure you call up your state animal control agencies and local police departments to thoroughly make sure that you are abiding all the rules if you still pursue animal ownership.

Before the actual purchase of your pet, make sure you have mingled with the pet beforehand. You need to be certain that you are compatible with ferrets, take time to get to know the traits of the ferret before the actual purchase.

You may go to a pet store that has them, you can also call up some ferret groups or even breeders and ask if you can mingle their pets for a short period of time.

Chapter Four: Acquiring a Ferret

You need to be able to stand the odor of the ferret. Since they belong in the Mustelidae family, they excrete odor if they believe that the situation is hazardous or harmful for them.

Most ferret owners say that their ferrets have a unique yet simple scent when they are calm, so you need to check up with your sense of smell before you pursue in buying a ferret.

Also check up if you can keep up with the energy level and playfulness of the pet. If you believe that you are overwhelmed with the antics of the ferrets when you are just visiting a pet owner, there is a big chance that you will be overwhelmed with having ferret as a permanent pet.

Think about buying ferrets in pairs. Ferrets are social beings and needs companion throughout the day. They can create a bond with other ferrets and they like having playmates whenever you are not around.

Some pet stores may even give you a discount when you buy a ferret in pairs. You may be charged with $75 for one ferret, but they might give you a bonded ferret for only $125.

Chapter Four: Acquiring a Ferret

Make sure you also look at your financial capability, see to it that you can afford not only to buy the pet but also to take care of the pet. The costs could jack up at any given moment.

Generally, you would spend around $100 - $150 for the ferret, but the supplies for the house of the ferret could be around $200 to $300.

Also check that you area able to treat several health problems when the need arises. Just like any other pet, your ferret needs yearly vaccines and examinations, so be prepared to shell out this kind of money for health care. Other than that, there might be some health issues in between these visits. These check - up and treatments add up to the cost of purchasing your pet, aside from giving it a good habitat and food to eat.

Just like any other dogs, your pet ferret need as yearly vaccine to treat rabies and distemper. The expense for this vaccine is around $150 to $200.

If you do not plan to breed your pet, you should spay or neuter it after you have bought it. This procedure would cost you around $100 to $250.

Chapter Four: Acquiring a Ferret

You should consider opening up an animal saving account. This account could be used during ferret emergency such as in surgeries or if it contracts a serious illness such as in cancer. If you put money in this account, make sure that this is all about your pet. The money put aside here would ease up your great burden of finding money when the need arises. It is easy to pull out cash rather than finding it where you can't find it.

Find also a vet that specializes in ferrets. Although vets consider problems of ferrets just like in cats, it is still best to find modern vet research that you should treat ferret separately and uniquely.

If you can't find vet area that specializes in ferret, find the nearest vet in your area and ask about his or her experience in dealing with ferrets.

Ready Your Home for the Storm

Having a ferret is unlike any other pet in the house. You could not just throw your ferret in your living room and let it be. You need to purchase a litter pan, cage, and litter for your pet.

Chapter Four: Acquiring a Ferret

Before you bring your pet home, you need to be sure that you have set up the toilet area and cage for your pet. Make sure that these areas are private but still your pet could easily acclimate itself.

Put a comfy bed inside the cage. Your pet ferret tend to sleep for 14 to 20 hours a day, so make sure that your pet could sleep all right in the bed. You can use an old shirt, sweatshirt, or even a sleeping tube from the pet store.

Do not use any wood shavings or cedar as bedding for your pet ferret. Although there are many pet stores that use this kind of bedding, dust could build up in the air which is definitely hazardous to your pet ferret.

The money for this task would be around $130, but this is only an initial expense.

Find the perfect leash, carrier, and collar. These things are used to transport your pet r even take your pet for a walk, for this task, you need to buy special supplies.

The carrier that you will buy must be well-ventilated. In the carrier, the floor should be solid panel; this will help your ferret have a stable surface underneath them. A great

Chapter Four: Acquiring a Ferret

alternative for ferret carriers are cat carriers, these are fairly cheap and will not hurt your budget.

Any collar and leash can be used by your ferret. You can use a leather puppy collar or even a nylon kitty collar; just make sure that the collar is not too tight for your pet.

Purchase a month's word of supply, as well as the food bowl and water bottle. There are many available pet ferret food found online or pet supply stores. If you have the budget, find the high protein, premium cat food you can afford.

The food dish should have a high, steep brim so your pet is not able to dig out of the food bowl. Your pet can drink from a water bottle, but they also like to drink it from a dish.

Cover any crevices and holes in your house. Go to your knees and look for any hidden holes in which your ferrets could get stuck in case that the burrow to.

See if there are any holes between the cabinet, under the ref, or even behind the laundry machine. Your pet might get stuck in these places and you might not see it immediately.

Chapter Four: Acquiring a Ferret

Use a wire mesh or wood to block holes from any area. Do not use any padded material or styrofoam, because these things can destroy and chew these materials.

Have latches or locks on all the drawers and cabinets. Your pet ferret is both dexterous and inquisitive, make sure you take time to ferret-proof your house immediately. Shelve and keep any hazardous materials immediately.

Have latches on your drawers. This will keep your ferret out and avoid rummaging, and aside from that, it could save the life of your pet. Ferrets are known to drink household solvents such as cleaning materials, make sure that you keep these dangerous toxins locked inside cabinets.

Staple all the hard - surfaced panel or any linoleum to the bottom of the bed or sofa. Your ferret could easily chew a hole in this soft-material furniture; this makes a good burrowing place. The damages in this furniture could be seriously dangerous for your pet. Make sure you protect all the bedding and mattresses.

Chapter Four: Acquiring a Ferret

Buying Your Pet Ferret

If you do not plan to breed your ferret, make sure you buy a ferret that is already spayed or neutered. This kind of pet will be around $100, you can buy these from private buyers or even private people.

Before you go off and buy in a store, make sure that you check first with the local animal shelter, because they have a lot of ferrets for your ready to adopt.

Before choosing the pet, make sure to check the tell - tale signs of your animal's health. Before sealing the deal, make sure that you are thoroughly sure that your pet is in great shape.

We have already discussed all the things you need to be in the lookout for the healthy ferret. Make sure that the pet is not sluggish or lethargic.

Ask the owner or person for certificates and records that is connected to your pet. In whatever place that you choose to buy your pet, make sure you obtain records and have these photocopied for your safekeeping.

Chapter Four: Acquiring a Ferret

Thoroughly know your pet before you even buy it, make sure that it already has vaccines and other treatments. Make sure that the records are up to date.

Look for the basic information sheet about your pet's weight, sex, age, de-scented, or spayed.

After purchasing the pet, immediately bring your pet for a check-up. The vet could help you ensure that the pet is safe and not bringing any diseases or any parasites inside the home. If possible, find a vet that specializes in ferrets.

Secure the permits and other records immediately. Keep these things in a safe place when emergency arises.

We have just given you the basics of purchasing your first ferret. Do not go off and rush to buy your first pet. Make sure that you thoroughly know your pet before you bring it home. Remember, it is better to be safe than sorry.

Chapter Four: Acquiring a Ferret

Chapter Five: Housing Requirements for Your Ferret

Ferrets are a unique companion that would surely spice up your home. They are very easy to train as well as learn new tricks that you would teach them. Some owners tell us that owning a ferret is just like owning a cat; however, your pet ferret still has its own unique characteristics that make your pet truly stand out. Due to its unique characteristics, you need to give the best for your pet. This chapter greatly deals with giving the best habitat for your pet ferret. A happy and healthy home contributes greatly to the longevity of the life of your pet.

Chapter Five: Housing Requirements for Your Ferret

Ferret Proofing 101

Your pet ferret is an intelligent, lively, fun-induced animal packed with a great deal of curiosity, due to its nature, sometimes, your pet could get in trouble.

This part will help you ferret proof your home to avoid any accidents involving not only your pet but also your home. You need to be patient and work your way through your home because you might miss a small spot.

To prevent accidents, you need to ferret-proof your home. To be sure that you will not miss any spots, you need to go down and dirty and see everything in the eyes of your pet.

Your pet is a fast, intelligent, and agile creatures, they can literally squeeze into even the smallest place possible. To avoid this, make sure to block any small gaps found under fire places, doors, boilers, radiators, back of kitchen appliances, freezes, fridges, or any big electronics. Your ferrets are very curious, they might get hurt, get stuck, or worse, be suffocated in the process.

Chapter Five: Housing Requirements for Your Ferret

Do not be complacent into thinking that a closed cabinet drawer and door could stop your curious ferret. This ferret would try everything to open a closed item! Make sure to child lock or even buy magnetic latches to keep sink cupboards and fridges completely closed. Make sure to keep away hazardous or even cleaning materials out of the reach of your pet.

Cables and wires make a fun game for your curious little pet. They like to bite through any electric cable, in turn, they might die due to electric shock, or worse, they could start a fire. Extension wires could be viewed by your pet as litter boxes, if your pet gets tempted, the urine could be seeped in the plug and start a fire. To prevent these accidents, you need to spray bitter apple or even rub fresh chilli on the wiring to help defer your pets.

You still need to keep all the wires out of reach of your pets; you might cover it with conduit, and secure your extension wires on to the walls.

Tumble dryers, washing machines, and dishwashers might be an ideal place for your pet ferret to go explore, start an adventure, and eventually fall asleep. And the least you

Chapter Five: Housing Requirements for Your Ferret

expected it, your ferret might be still inside when you use and turn on these appliances.

If you have time and money, you might opt to buy carpet and cut it into pieces. These pieces would then be use to cover holes using a carpet tape. It might not look very pretty but it will prevent the unnecessary light that would entice your pet to go and explore it.

However, your pet might be enticed to go out and poo and pee on these pieces so your carpet pieces might get smelly and stained over time. You need to habitually replace your carpet to prevent the foul odor in your home. You can also clean your carpet regularly in machines, or you could also use sprays in between cleans.

If you want your pet ferret to stay in only one place but you still want to access different areas in your house. You need to put up barriers taller and higher than your ferrets to jump into, but low enough for you to be able to cross it.

For your bathrooms, you need to keep the lid down in your toilet as your pet may fall into and they may drown.

Chapter Five: Housing Requirements for Your Ferret

The buttons on your remote and even small rubbers are a great treat for your ferret, so they might like to chew these things. Unfortunately, your ferret can't digest the rubber and will just block their bowels, this will kill your ferret if you do not spot it early enough. This is the same with foams such as in your mattresses and even headphone covers.

Another great trait of your ferret is that they like to climb and jump up to even three feet! This characteristic will make them eager to find their way up especially if they smell something delicious.

Drawers, sofas, chairs, and even tables are great ladders for your pet. Boxes and any other similar shaped objects will help them go up to higher places. Even though they are great climbers, your pet might have a hard time getting down from high places. This would lead to injury especially if they fall from a great height. Make sure that high areas are unreachable and do not leave your pet unsupervised especially at rooms where your pet could have places to climb.

Chapter Five: Housing Requirements for Your Ferret

Since your pet is very flexible and small, your pet might get squashed in between chairs an sofas, especially if someone sits on the cushion and not see your pet lounging over there. Do not even think of buying a recliner if you plan to have a pet ferret. There are several reports of ferrets death due to suffocation, killed, and even maimed in between the recliners.

If you have fuel or wood burner/stove or even an open fire place, you need to put a safety fireguard. These fireguards are the ones with enclosure on the top and the sides. Make sure to secure it every time. This procedure would prevent your pet from getting accidentally burned when in use, aside from that; this will prevent your pet from exploring the chimney when you are not using it. Remember, these safeguards will get hot too for your ferret, so make sure to always supervise your ferret when it is near the fire. See to it that your ferret can't go through the guard and their claws will not get stuck to it.

House plants are a gray area for your pet. Your ferret might spend time digging it out, so if you plan to have

Chapter Five: Housing Requirements for Your Ferret

plants in your house with ferrets around, make sure that the plant is not poisonous for your ferret.

These are some house plants that look fine, but are terrible and be poisonous to your pet ferret:

- Aloe Vera
- Castor Oil Plants
- Lillies
- Crocus
- English Ivy
- Pointsettia
- Rhubarb
- Cocoa Shell Mulch.
- Aloe Vera
- African Violet
- Amaryllis
- Apple (seeds)
- Apple Leaf Croton
- Apricot (pit)
- Asparagus Fern
- Autumn Crocus

- Azalea
- Baby's Breath
- Begonia Rex
- Bird of Paradise
- Bittersweet
- Branching Ivy
- Buckeye
- Buddhist Pine
- Caladium
- Calla Lily
- Castor Bean
- Century Plant
- Ceriman
- Charming Dieffenbachia

Chapter Five: Housing Requirements for Your Ferret

- ✓ Cherry (seeds and wilting leaves)
- ✓ Chinese Evergreen
- ✓ Chrysanthemum
- ✓ Cineraria
- ✓ Clematis
- ✓ Cordatum
- ✓ Corn Plant
- ✓ Cornstalk Plant
- ✓ Croton
- ✓ Cuban Laurel
- ✓ Cutleaf Philodendron
- ✓ Cycads
- ✓ Cyclamen
- ✓ Daffodil
- ✓ Devil's Ivy
- ✓ Dieffenbachia
- ✓ Dracaena Palm
- ✓ Dragon Tree
- ✓ Dumb Cane
- ✓ Easter Lily
- ✓ Elaine
- ✓ Elephant Ears
- ✓ Emerald Feather
- ✓ English Ivy
- ✓ Eucalyptus
- ✓ Fiddle-leaf Fig
- ✓ Florida Beauty
- ✓ Four O' Clock
- ✓ Foxglove
- ✓ Fruit Salad Plant
- ✓ Geranium
- ✓ German Ivy
- ✓ Giant Dumb Cane
- ✓ Glacier Ivy
- ✓ Gold Dust Dracaena
- ✓ Golden Pathos
- ✓ Hahn's Self- Branching Ivy
- ✓ Heartland Philodendron
- ✓ Hurricane Plant

Chapter Five: Housing Requirements for Your Ferret

- ✓ Hydrangea
- ✓ Indian Rubber Plant
- ✓ Iris
- ✓ Ivy (English and Baltic)
- ✓ Janet Craig Dracaena
- ✓ Japanese Show Lily
- ✓ Jerusalem Cherry
- ✓ Jimsom Weed
- ✓ Kalanchoe
- ✓ Lacy Tree Philodendron
- ✓ Lily of the Valley
- ✓ Madagascar Dragon Tree
- ✓ Marble Queen
- ✓ Marigold
- ✓ Marijuana
- ✓ Mexican Breadfruit
- ✓ Miniature Croton
- ✓ Mistletoe
- ✓ Morning Glory
- ✓ Mother-in Law's Tongue
- ✓ Narcissus
- ✓ Needlepoint Ivy
- ✓ Nephytis
- ✓ Nightshade
- ✓ Oleander
- ✓ Onion
- ✓ Oriental Lily
- ✓ Peace Lily
- ✓ Peach (wilting leaves and pits)
- ✓ Pencil Cactus
- ✓ Peperonia
- ✓ Petunia
- ✓ Philodendron
- ✓ Plumosa Fern
- ✓ Poinsettia (low toxicity)
- ✓ Poison Ivy
- ✓ Poison Hemlock
- ✓ Poison Oak

Chapter Five: Housing Requirements for Your Ferret

- ✓ Potato (sprouts)
- ✓ Pothos
- ✓ Prayer Plant
- ✓ Precatory Bean
- ✓ Primrose
- ✓ Red Emerald
- ✓ Red Princess
- ✓ Red-Margined Dracaena
- ✓ Rhododendron
- ✓ Rhubarb leaf blades
- ✓ Ribbon Plant
- ✓ Rubber Plant
- ✓ Saddle Leaf Philodendron
- ✓ Sago Palm
- ✓ Satin Pothos
- ✓ Schefflera
- ✓ Silver Pothos
- ✓ Spotted Dumb Cane
- ✓ String of Pearls
- ✓ Striped Dracaena
- ✓ Sweet violets
- ✓ Sweetheart Ivy
- ✓ Swiss Cheese Plant
- ✓ Taro Vine
- ✓ Thorn Apple
- ✓ Tiger Lily
- ✓ Tomato Plant (green fruit stem and leaves)
- ✓ Tree Philodendron
- ✓ Tropic Snow
- ✓ Dieffenbachia
- ✓ Tulips
- ✓ Weeping Fig
- ✓ Wormwood
- ✓ Yew

Chapter Five: Housing Requirements for Your Ferret

Other household hazards include:

- ✓ Ant baits
- ✓ Silica gel packets (found in delivery packaging, bag and even in some furniture)
- ✓ Potpurri
- ✓ Essential oils
- ✓ Chocolate, Raisins
- ✓ Sultanas
- ✓ Nuts
- ✓ Cigarettes
- ✓ Bread Dough
- ✓ Mothballs
- ✓ Rat/Mice Poisons
- ✓ Antifreeze Human medicines
- ✓ Asprin
- ✓ Nurofen
- ✓ Ibuprofen
- ✓ Paracetamol
- ✓ Warfarin
- ✓ Cleaning products

Chapter Five: Housing Requirements for Your Ferret

- ✓ Bleach
- ✓ Detergents
- ✓ Household Cleaning Sprays
- ✓ Polish
- ✓ The things that you typically keep under the sink.

Your pet ferret only needs a few licks from a nozzle, or even a small lap from a pool of detergent, and your ferret would surely die. Your ferret is so smart that it could open child-resistant bottles or even chew the heavy plastic containers. Make sure that you stow these away and lock 'em up! These things should not be lying around or be used around when your ferret is around.

Do not even try to give your ferret any OTC medications or prescription medicines without checking with the vet first. Just like any other animals, your pet ferret could be easily killed and be poisoned by using common human medications.

Your food with really look yummy to your ferret; however, it will not be good for your pet! Make sure that the food is surely be out of your pet's reach.

Chapter Five: Housing Requirements for Your Ferret

Just like any other animals, wash your hands before and after handling food and before and after handling your ferret. Your ferret might accidentally bite you. Your pet might not realize it until it has sunken its teeth on your skin, and realize that it is not food.

Sometimes, your ferret may disappear when you let it loose in your house. If it disappears for a period of time, make sure to listen to any rustling or scratching noises inside the house. Aside from that, make sure to look for dark and snuggly places, such as in the bottom of the wardrobes, drawers, washing machines, and etc. These are some places where your ferret could sleep.

Other than that, make sure to teach your ferret a call signal noise, such as a squeak of a toy, rattling of the pack of treats, in which your ferret could respond to, if it successfully responds, make sure to reward your pet with a treat!

A good rule of thumb is that if you do not want to lose a thing, make sure you hide it very well from your ferret.

Chapter Five: Housing Requirements for Your Ferret

Ferret - Proofing Your Garden

Your ferret likes to burrow, jump, and climb, and they could even squeeze to any gap that they could find! They would like to go through the gates and fences. Aside from ferret proofing your home, it is better that you also ferret proof your garden, this may be a big challenge and you will not get it write at the first try.

Climbing 101

Since your ferret likes to climb around, make sure that the fence around your garden is smooth. This will stop your ferret to climb and try to escape to the other side and potentially hurt itself.

Your ferret could even climb a wall if they have ridges and cracks or if it is covered in pebble dash, so if possible, make sure that you smooth over the cracks and ridges to prevent your pet from climbing out.

You may use stiff plastic sheet, such as corrugated plastic roofing sheet, galvanized sheet metal, recycled glass

Chapter Five: Housing Requirements for Your Ferret

doors or woods, plywood or even fibre - cement fencing sheets.

If your fence has no gap in between them, you just need to ferret-proof the under the ground. Dig a small trench below the fence and use any of the aforementioned materials, alongside with treated wooden sleepers, filling it with cement or even concrete paving slabs.

Some owners even say that their ferrets can climb brick walls, so make sure that there is a sheet metal or plastic that is around 30 cm high. Secure it along the length of the way at around 1m or above. Create a simple overhang above the fence to prevent your ferret to snoop and try to visit the other side.

The fencing material should go beyond two to three feet under, along with four feet above ground level.

If you can't ferret proof your garden, secure a small area for your pet to play in. Although make sure that there are no holes in which your pet could go through.

You should ferret-proof the whole outside area rather than separating your pet. It is noted that ferrets and humans love to bond each other and likes to play with each other!

Chapter Five: Housing Requirements for Your Ferret

Ground covers and shrubs, however, you need to keep away vines, ivy, shrubs, and trees away from the edges of the fence. If you have trees in your garden, cover the trunk with plastic and tightly screw it in to have a barrier against your ferret from ever climbing it.

If your pet can freely roam inside the garden, make sure that there is no open ponds in which your pet could swim into. If you have ponds, make sure that there is a sloping pond that could help your pet return to their original state.

Make sure you securely cover any water butts and your pet ferret can't access the downpipe from the gutter to the butt. See to it that the drainage holes are covered with grids so your pet could not fall over or even wander off to it.

You can still have a pond for the warmer month if you take into consideration your pet. The edges should be low if ever your pet decides to swim, just make sure that your pet could climb out easily. You could also use plastic baby pool as ponds. However, put bricks in the water to help your pet step out of the pond.

Chapter Five: Housing Requirements for Your Ferret

Tips

To have a happy pet, you must provide a happy home for your pet ferret. Here are some quick tips to create a conducive while still happy environment for your pet:

- ✓ Remember that your ferret likes to explore in your house, this would result in your pet getting into trouble.

- ✓ Your pet could easily chew and swallow any small materials such as cloth, rubber, and vinyl.

- ✓ They also like to jump, climb, and get themselves stuck in between objects especially when they try to escape.

- ✓ Purchase a cage with an escape proof latch for safekeeping. Some stores carry 2 to 3 storey cages are very idea.

Chapter Five: Housing Requirements for Your Ferret

- ✓ Your ferret likes to have roomy cages; it should be around 30 to 36 inches long, 16 to 18 inches wide, with 18 inches of ceiling height.

- ✓ You need to have washable pet rugs because your pet is not really used to walking on wires.

- ✓ The cage should be in a shaded, cool, dry area away from direct sunlight.

- ✓ Your pet could easily die from heat stroke if the temperature is more than 80 degrees Fahrenheit.

- ✓ You should not leave your pet ferret for a long period of time inside the cage. Your pet needs exercise, companionship, and love every day.

- ✓ Your pet ferret can sleep around 15 to 20 hours a day; make sure that there is a comfortable sleeping area for your pet. If they can't find a comfortable bed, your pet will dig everywhere to find the most comfy one.

Chapter Five: Housing Requirements for Your Ferret

- ✓ You can use hammocks, pet blankets, and even synthetic lambswool centers, and even small pet beds can be used as pet beds.

- ✓ You should not use cedar chips as bedding as this will pose as a great big respiratory risk to your pet ferret. Any wood chips could absorb musk, urine, and waste odor and nothing can ever mask these smelly smell.

- ✓ Make sure to change the bedding every other day to prevent unnecessary odors.

- ✓ You should not use fabric softeners or even perfumed detergents to wash your pet's bedding because some ferrets are allergic to the scent of these things.

- ✓ You should immediately litter train your pet as soon as you got them. Litter training requires great time, techniques, products, patience, and even positive reinforcement.

Chapter Five: Housing Requirements for Your Ferret

- ✓ You can use plant fibres or even recycled newspapers as your litter products. These things are dust-free, super absorbent, truly non allergenic, longer tray lives, and environmentally friendly.

- ✓ The typical clay litters are not really suitable for your pet ferret. These things may cause your pet's coat to be brittle and dry; this dust could cause a problem in their upper respiratory system.

- ✓ You can use a plastic litter pan alongside metal or plastic poop scoop. These things work well.

- ✓ You should not use rubber or soft latex dog and cat toys because they might chew and swallow them. These things cause big intestinal blockage for your ferret and could potentially lead to your ferret's death.

- ✓ Safe toys include hard rubber balls with bells inside, cat taser toys, washable cat crinkle tunnels. You can even buy a pet tunnel and tent for your pet to sleep in.

Chapter Five: Housing Requirements for Your Ferret

These are some things that can potentially help you in building the best house for your pet ferret. However, this is only a brief overview about the ferret housing. You could still do a thorough research to fully know the specs of the ferret house

Chapter Five: Housing Requirements for Your Ferret

Chapter Six: Food and Nutrition for Your Pet Ferret

Just like any other humans, your pet ferret needs a complete and healthy nutrition to be able to function well. A pet needs to have a complete meal to have a happy life as well to have a healthy body. Since your ferret is a fairly active animal, you should greatly consider this characteristic. Make sure that you set a feeding time and frequency so that your pet will get used to the process of eating. This chapter will help you understand what your pet ferret eats on a daily basis. Choose the best food for your pet.

Chapter Six: Food and Nutrition for Your Pet Ferret

Ferret Nutrition 101

Research is the key. If you do not know anything about your pet ferret, make sure you do thorough research to construct the best nutritional diet needed by your pet ferret. There are a lot of websites that could help you in personalizing your pet's diet.

What and When Will My Ferret Eat?

To simply put it, your ferret has a high and fast metabolism. In reality, you need to feed your pet ferret around eight to 10 small meals every day. Just like cats, your pet ferrets are strictly carnivores, which mean they need to have a high protein diet. Some owners tend to choose cat food, but do not choose the fish variety.

Food pellets are a top choice for your pet ferrets. This food type is typically found in a local pet store or even in your vet's office.

Chapter Six: Food and Nutrition for Your Pet Ferret

To be a good pet owner, you need to read the ingredients on the packet. This is to ensure that you will get the most nutritious ingredients needed by your pet ferret.

As the rule of thumb, the ingredients on the list are ordered from highest to lowest quantity. Also, you should find food that is high in chicken or even lamb. But, do not feed your ferret anything that has corn or grain.

What if I Can't Find Ferret Specific Food?

Sometimes, pet stores or vet stores do not carry specific ferret food. But do not be afraid, kitten food could work well for your ferret. To do this, you must check the ingredients list on the packet. The ingredient should contain fatty acid supplements. Remember, kitten food has a higher protein inside rather than the adult cat food. In this essence, kitten food is better for your pet ferret.

Chapter Six: Food and Nutrition for Your Pet Ferret

Are There Any Food I Can Give My Pet Ferret?

If you have time, you can cook homemade meal to feed your ferret. You can choose between raw or cooked chicken, along with pellets.

You can also give chicken baby food as a supplement for the pellet diet. However, you must keep in mind that dry food is must to keep your pet ferret's teeth clean.

Any Foods To Avoid?

Just like any animals, your pet has certain food restrictions. You should not give food that is high in complex carbohydrates. Some examples of these things are vegetables, fruits, dairy, or any food that has sugar in it. Remember, you pet ferret is a carnivore, which means it can't process these kinds of foods. Here are some other foods that you should not give to your pet ferret:

✓ Dairy
✓ Onions and garlics

Chapter Six: Food and Nutrition for Your Pet Ferret

- ✓ Grains
- ✓ Xylitol
- ✓ Dog food
- ✓ Cooked bones
- ✓ Chocolate
- ✓ Candy
- ✓ Peas

Varied Health to Have Healthy Body

Just like any other animals, your ferret can be picky eaters. They might even prefer one food over the other. So it is best to have a variety of food to give to your pet. Or you can switch up brands from time to time.

If you have a picky eater, try to mix small amounts of new food in the old food until your pet have transitioned well to the new food. This task may take around two weeks.

If you choose ferret pellet, you need to inspect the shape of the pellet carefully. If the shape of the pellet is sharp, such as triangles, these things could jab the roof of your pet ferret's mouth. So choose the ones that are small yet smooth chunks, oval shaped food are also preferred.

Watch Out For the Hairballs

Your ferret is self - cleaning animals. In this case, they might get hairballs. However, your pet ferret can't and don't regurgitate hairballs unlike your cats. To fight this problem, there are manufacturers that have created treats to prevent hairballs from ever developing. Add these specialized treats to your pet's diet and even weekly routine.

If, unfortunately, your ferret ingests some hairball that has lodged in its body, you need to take it to your vet immediately to have it surgically removed. Remember, it is better to prevent this incident that to cure it.

Chapter Six: Food and Nutrition for Your Pet Ferret

Smart (and Healthy) Treats

Your ferret likes treats. Some good treats for your pet includes:

- ✓ Cat treats
- ✓ Cooked eggs
- ✓ Bits of chicken
- ✓ Pieces of lamb
- ✓ Turkey

However, as we have said, you should not give vegetable, grains, ice cream or even chocolate. Stick with treats specifically made for ferrets, however, if you could not find treats for ferrets, find treats for cats, but do not give dog treats!

A great tip is to befriend the butcher and ask for organs or other parts that people do not really like to buy but your ferret would like. However, make sure that the pieces of meat are fresh! To avoid any diseases and illnesses, make sure to cook the meat thoroughly before you give it to your pet ferret.

Chapter Six: Food and Nutrition for Your Pet Ferret

A thing you can do is cook a big bunch at a time and store it into freezer. Cut up a small amount then thaw in the microwave. Easy, right?

These are just some reminders on what your ferret likes to eat on a daily basis. However, this is just the beginning of a happy and healthy journey with your new best friend, your pet ferret.

Chapter Seven: Ferret Grooming 101

Grooming your pet is an essential task that you need to do almost daily. Even though your pet could potentially clean itself, it is still better to thoroughly check what the state of your pet. Grooming could also make you see the potential problems of your pet. You can find signs and symptoms of illnesses early on.

You might think that your ferret is small, so it is generally easy to groom. However, their bodies need basic maintenance and grooming. As we have said before, ferrets

Chapter Seven: Ferret Grooming 101

are self-cleaning animals; however, you should also inspect what they have done to give them the best and to make them the best they could ever be. Here are some basic grooming techniques that you need to do for your ferret:

Brushing Teeth

Remember, you should regularly brush your ferret's teeth. If you give chunkier or softer food for his diet, he might need to have his teeth brushed more frequently, just like once a week than a ferret that eats dry food. Brushing might be traumatic for your pet ferret, just like any other animals at the first try. Your pet ferret will soon adjust after a few tries coupled with your patience.

- Make sure that you use a pet toothpaste and toothbrush. Slowly brush your teeth from the back up to the front.

- Pay close attention to clean the molars of your pet. In this area, there are a lot of plaque and tartar build -

up. The reason for this is the ferret's tongue can't really clean the things off the teeth.

Even if you clean the teeth regularly, you still need to have your pet ferret's teeth professionally cleaned every one to three years or even more.

Cleaning Ears

You should clean your pet ferret's ear weekly to prevent any kind of prevent, unpleasant odor, and even ear mites.

- You need to use a commercial ear cleaning solution, this should be recommended by your vet, put a few warm drops into your ferret's eat and massage the pet's ear to work the inside of the ear.

- Using the ear drops would loosen any wax inside the ear. You still need to remove the loosened wax using a damp Q - tip.

Chapter Seven: Ferret Grooming 101

It is near to impossible to injure your pet ferret's ear drum because it is L shaped, however, you should still clean the ear gently. Continue cleaning the ear until the Q-tip comes out clean. You might need to constantly change your q-tip from time to time.

Clipping Nails

You should clip your pet ferret's nails around twice a month. Clipping the nail would avoid the snagging that might cause to accidentally rip off the nail.

Before the nail clipping agenda, you should ready all the materials first. The materials needed for this task is ferret or cat nail clipper, styptic powder (this is used if you need to cut the nail too close, and your pet ferret's treat - to assure that your pet will cooperate.

- Place your pet ferret on the back your lap, also place some treat on his belly, while he is eating the treat, slowly clip the nails.

Chapter Seven: Ferret Grooming 101

- The clipped nail should be parallel to the floor when he is walking or standing, do not cut too quick or near the pink vein of the nail.

- If you have ever cut this pink vein, put some styptic powder on your pet ferret's nail to stop the bleeding.

Bathing

Bathing is essential to any living being. On the other hand, over bathing is very bad for your pet. If you over - bathe your pet, it may cause dry skin, it will make him uncomfortable and itchy, thus, he will secrete his musky odor.

If you plan on bathing you pet, make sure you use a shampoo specifically designed for your pet ferret, the pH balance should agree with its ski.

- Ready a tub with warm water, your ferret has a steady body temperature of 102, so lukewarm water might be too much for your pet ferret.

Chapter Seven: Ferret Grooming 101

- To test the deepness of the water, your pet ferret's head should be well above the water.

- Shampoo and lather the bubbles generously, then rinse thoroughly.

- Make sure that there no soap left in the coat, for this will dry out your pet's body and skin.

- Make sure to thoroughly pat dry your pet ferret, lay your pet on a bunched up towel. Your pet ferret would dry himself through rolling and tossing around.

Photo Credits

Page 10 Photo by user Christels via Pixabay.com,

https://pixabay.com/en/ferret-white-sheet-domestic-animal-1970169/

Page 13 Photo by user MichaelSehlmeyer via Pixabay.com

https://pixabay.com/en/animals-ferret-animal-welfare-1144845/

Page 32 Photo by user Skeeze via Pixabay.com,

https://pixabay.com/en/black-footed-ferrets-looking-two-967192/

Page 57 Photo by user Christels via Pixabay.com,

https://pixabay.com/en/ferret-animal-close-up-1880601/

Page 76 Photo by user Christels via Pixabay.com,

https://pixabay.com/en/ferret-yawn-language-1972523/

Page 101 Photo by user Christels via Pixabay.com,

https://pixabay.com/en/ferret-animal-domestic-1974374/

Page 110 Photo by user Christels via Pixabay.com,

https://pixabay.com/en/ferret-animal-grass-close-up-1871994/

Page 110 Photo by user Pipsimv via Pixabay.com,

https://pixabay.com/en/ferret-animal-eyes-close-up-361577/

References

History of the Ferret – WeaselWords.com

https://weaselwords.com/ferret-articles/history-of-the-ferret/

Pros and Cons of Ferrets as Pets – Mom.me

https://animals.mom.me/pros-cons-ferrets-pets-5059.html

Ferrets – Seniorlink.co.nz

http://www.seniorlink.co.nz/interests/pets/ferret.shtml

Ferret Care Sheet - Kraftmobilevet.com

https://kraftmobilevet.com/wp-content/uploads/2017/10/ferret-care.pdf

Your Healthy Happy Ferret – Petco.com

https://www.petco.com/content/petco/PetcoStore/en_US/pet-services/resource-center/health-wellness/Your-Healthy-Happy-Ferret.html

Buying a Ferret – WikiHow.com

https://www.wikihow.com/Buy-a-Ferret

Ferret Housing Tips – Petcha.com

https://www.petcha.com/ferret-housing-tips/

Ferret Proofing – FerretInfo.co.uk

http://ferretinfo.co.uk/ferret-proofing/4541132359

Providing a Home for a Ferret - Merckvetmanual.com

https://www.merckvetmanual.com/en-ca/all-other-pets/ferrets/providing-a-home-for-a-ferret

Nutrition for Your Ferret – PetMD.com

https://www.petmd.com/ferret/nutrition/evr_ft_nutrition_ferret

How to Groom a Ferret – Ferret.com

https://www.ferret.com/ferret-articles/how-to-groom-a-ferret/7/

www.ingramcontent.com/pod-product-compliance
Lightning Source LLC
Chambersburg PA
CBHW071954070426
42453CB00008BA/790